Gr 3-41

Michigan

Niels R. Jensen

Visit us at
www.abdopublishing.com

Editor: John Hamilton
Graphic Design: Sue Hamilton
Cover Illustration: Neil Klinepier
Cover Photo: iStock Photo

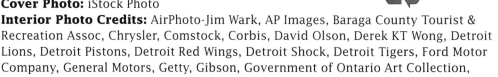

Manufactured with paper containing at least 10% post-consumer waste

Interior Photo Credits: AirPhoto-Jim Wark, AP Images, Baraga County Tourist & Recreation Assoc, Chrysler, Comstock, Corbis, David Olson, Derek KT Wong, Detroit Lions, Detroit Pistons, Detroit Red Wings, Detroit Shock, Detroit Tigers, Ford Motor Company, General Motors, Getty, Gibson, Government of Ontario Art Collection, Granger Collection, Gunter Küchler, iStock Photo, Kellogg Company, Kraft Foods-Post Cereals, Library of Congress, Michigan Historical Center, Michigan Dept of Transportation, Mile High Maps, Mountain High Maps, NASA, North American International Auto Show, One Mile Up, and Peter Arnold Inc.
Statistics: State population statistics taken from 2008 U.S. Census Bureau estimates. City and town population statistics taken from July 1, 2007, U.S. Census Bureau estimates. Land and water area statistics taken from 2000 Census, U.S. Census Bureau.

Library of Congress Cataloging-in-Publication Data

Jensen, Niels R., 1949-
  Michigan / Niels R. Jensen.
      p. cm. -- (The United States)
  Includes index.
  ISBN 978-1-60453-657-7
  1. Michigan--Juvenile literature. I. Title.

  F566.3.J46 2009
  977.4--dc22

                              2008051702

Table of Contents

The Wolverine State

Michigan is an unusual state. It is far inland, but has the longest coastline of any state, except Alaska. That is because four of the five Great Lakes nearly surround it.

Thanks to Michigan's waterways, fur traders made huge fortunes in the 1700s and 1800s. Today, nearly 90 million tons (82 million metric tons) of freight pass through the river ports at Sault Sainte Marie each year.

After the fur trade declined around 1840, the region turned to lumbering, mining, and farming. In the 1900s, many automobile manufacturers came to the state.

Michigan is known as the Wolverine State because of an argument with the state of Ohio over a piece of land. The people of Ohio thought the Michiganians were as ornery as wolverines. The name stuck.

Canoers pass Eagle Harbor Lighthouse on Michigan's Upper Peninsula.

Quick Facts

Name: Michigan may come from an Ojibwe Native American word, *mishigama*, which means "large or great lake."

State Capital: Lansing, population 114,947

Date of Statehood: January 26, 1837 (26th state)

Population: 10,003,422 (8th-most populous state)

Area (Total Land and Water): 97,790 square miles (253,275 sq km), 11th-largest state

Largest City: Detroit, population 916,952

Nicknames: Wolverine State, Great Lakes State

Motto: *Si quaeris peninsulam amoenam circumspice* (If you seek a pleasant peninsula, look about you)

State Bird: Robin

State Flower: Apple Blossom

State Rock: Petoskey Stone

State Tree: White Pine

State Song: "My Michigan"

Highest Point: Mount Arvon, 1,979 feet (603 m)

Lowest Point: Lake Erie, 571 feet (174 m)

Average July Temperature: 69°F (21°C)

Record High Temperature: 112°F (44°C), Mio, July 13, 1936

Average January Temperature: 19°F (-7°C)

Record Low Temperature: -51°F (-46°C), Vanderbilt, February 9, 1934

Average Annual Precipitation: 31 inches (79 cm)

Number of U.S. Senators: 2

Number of U.S. Representatives: 15

U.S. Postal Service Abbreviation: MI

Geography

Michigan is split between two land areas known as the Lower and Upper Peninsulas. They are each very unique.

The Upper Peninsula is rocky, mountainous, and swampy. It is sometimes called the Superior Upland. Large copper and iron deposits are found there. It is also heavily forested. Some parts are still wilderness. The Huron Mountains is one such area. Here is found Mount Arvon, the highest point in the state.

The Lower Peninsula is made up of sedimentary rocks. The soils of the Lower Peninsula are very fertile, especially in the south. There are many farms in the region.

Isle Royale is the northernmost part of Michigan. This remote island group has been a national park since 1940. It is only accessible by boat or float plane.

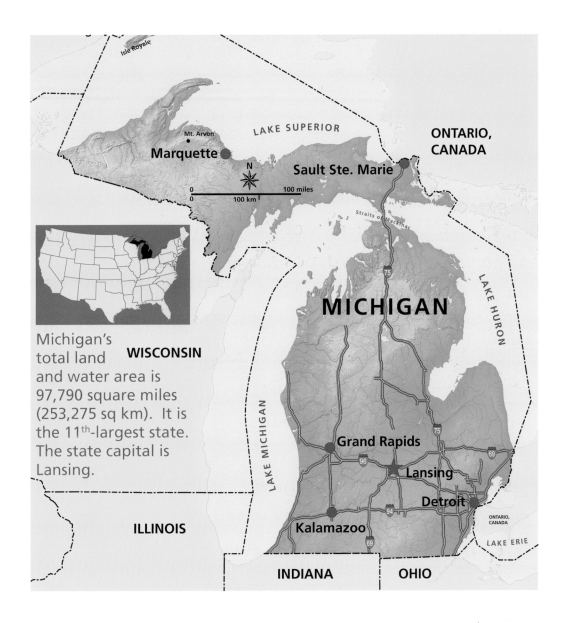

Isle Royale

LAKE SUPERIOR

Mt. Arvon

Marquette

Sault Ste. Marie

ONTARIO, CANADA

N

0   100 miles
0   100 km

Straits of Mackinac

75

MICHIGAN

LAKE HURON

Michigan's total land and water area is 97,790 square miles (253,275 sq km). It is the 11ᵗʰ-largest state. The state capital is Lansing.

WISCONSIN

LAKE MICHIGAN

Grand Rapids

96

75

69

★ **Lansing**

94

Detroit

ONTARIO, CANADA

Kalamazoo

69

LAKE ERIE

ILLINOIS

INDIANA   **OHIO**

Water from ice age glaciers created the Great Lakes. About 4,000 years ago, Michigan's connecting channels of the Detroit River, St. Mary's River, and Straits of Mackinac formed.

Aerial view of the Great Lakes.

Today, they are all part of the St. Lawrence Seaway.

The Straits of Mackinac run between Michigan's Upper and Lower Peninsulas. In 1957, the Mackinac Bridge was built connecting the two peninsulas. Spanning a distance of five miles (eight km), it is one of the longest suspension bridges in the world. It is sometimes called the Big Mac or Mighty Mac.

Michigan shares borders with Indiana, Ohio, Wisconsin, and Ontario, Canada. Detroit is the only major city in the United States where you can travel south into Canada.

A tall ship passes beneath the Mackinac Bridge near Mackinaw City, Michigan.

Climate and Weather

While Michigan is nearly surrounded by the Great Lakes, its inland location brings hot summers and cold winters. The state's daytime temperatures are usually in the upper

On hot summer days, people come to Michigan's beaches to cool off.

70s and lower 80s degrees Fahrenheit (mid- to upper-20s degrees C) during the summer.

Evaporation from the Great Lakes causes Michigan to have more cloudy days than most other states. The Upper Peninsula sees huge amounts of lake effect snow in winter.

A pier and lighthouse is engulfed in the waters from Lake Michigan. Some storms bring near hurricane-force winds to the area.

Great Lakes shipping is affected by the gales that sometimes blow through the state. These strong winds can even sink modern freighters. In November 1975, the 729-foot (222-m) *Edmund Fitzgerald* was hit by a violent gale on Lake Superior. The ship sank and all 29 crewmen died.

In winter, some Michigan waters freeze. Even large ships equipped with icebreakers may not be able to keep the shipping lanes open. The ice may begin to form in December, and may not melt until May.

Plants and Animals

Michigan has prairies, southern forests, boreal forests, shorelines, dunes, and wetlands. Many different plants and animals live in these habitats.

About 100 years ago, Michigan was the nation's leading supplier of lumber. Huge wooded areas were cut down. Today, about half the state is still forested. About two-thirds of these trees are birch, aspen, and oak. Black spruce is found in the state's northern bogs. Northern pin oak and jack pine grow in sandy areas.

Michigan is famous for its cherry trees. The apple blossom is the state flower.

A cherry tree orchard in Michigan.

Deer are common in Michigan's forests.

Deer are plentiful in Michigan. Other animals include bear, wolf, elk, fox, moose, and bobcats.

Although Michigan is known as the Wolverine State, the wolverine is rarely seen today. In 2004, a wolverine was spotted in the village of Ubly. It was the first such sighting in 200 years.

Birds in Michigan include the bald eagle, as well as pheasants, ducks, geese, grouse, hawks, loons, quail, swans, wild turkeys, and Kirtland's warblers.

The rare Kirtland's warbler lives in the jack pine forests of Michigan.

The waters of Michigan are full of fish, including bass, muskellunge, northern pike, perch, salmon, smelt, steelhead, sturgeon, trout, and walleye.

Black bears are found in Michigan's forests.

Moose

Gray Wolf

Hawk

History

In the early 1600s, the first French explorers came to what is now Michigan. Frenchman Etienne Brule explored the area from 1618-1622.

Several Native American tribes lived in Michigan.

Most of the area's Native Americans were part of the Council of the Three Fires. This included the Chippewa (Ojibwe), Ottawa, and Potawatomi tribes. Other tribes in the area included the Huron (Wyandot), Mascouten, Menominee, and Miami.

The first real sailing ship on the Great Lakes arrived in 1679. The *Griffin* was a French cargo ship. It sailed through Lake Erie, and up the Detroit River to Lake Huron and Lake Michigan. Loaded with furs in Wisconsin, the ship began a return voyage east. It was never seen again.

In 1701, Antoine de la Mothe Cadillac landed in Detroit with 100 men, including his young son and two missionaries.

The city of Detroit had its beginning in 1701, when Antoine de la Mothe Cadillac built Fort Pontchartrain du Détroit. The small settlement quickly grew into an important fur trading post.

Wars arose between France and Great Britain, as each side tried to claim the region. American colonists won their independence from Great Britain during the Revolutionary War (1775-1783).

The city of Detroit began to grow once the Erie Canal opened. People could travel westward across New York state to the Great Lakes.

In 1805, Michigan Territory was created. Settlement was slow until 1825, when the Erie Canal opened. This waterway brought people across New York state to the Great Lakes.

In 1833, Michigan asked for statehood, but it failed in Congress. Southern slave states were against the admission of another free state. Ohio was against the proposed boundary of Michigan.

In 1835, a border dispute between Ohio and Michigan centered on a  468-square-mile (1,212-sq-km) area that included the city of Toledo. Governors of both areas gathered troops, ready to fight. President Andrew Jackson and the U.S. Congress stepped in and stopped the Toledo War.

Ohio was given the Toledo Strip. Michigan received the Upper Peninsula. At the time, some people in Michigan felt they had been cheated. They were proved wrong when vast resources of copper, iron, and lumber were discovered in the Upper Peninsula.

Stevens Mason was called the "Boy Governor."

Michigan finally received statehood on January 26, 1837. It became the 26th state in the Union. At 24 years of age, Stevens T. Mason became the state's first and youngest governor. The state capital began in Detroit, but moved to Lansing in 1847.

In 1861, the American Civil War began. A strong anti-slavery state, Michigan supported the Union with more than 90,000 troops. Runaway slaves were helped by the Underground Railroad. Laura Smith Haviland opened one of the first schools in Michigan to admit African American children. Sojourner Truth, a freed slave, spoke to hundreds of people. The North won the war in 1865.

In the 1900s, Michigan's farms and industries grew along with the state's population. Ships and railroads transported huge loads of copper, iron, and lumber. Furniture making and food processing developed. Detroit emerged as the automotive business center of the nation.

The Purple Gang

In 1920, the 18th Amendment went into effect. This made it illegal to brew and sell alcohol in the United States. Criminals brought illegal alcohol from Canada across Michigan's border. Detroit's Purple Gang were especially ruthless.

The 21st Amendment ended the ban on alcohol in 1933. Michigan was the first state to approve it.

During World War I and World War II, Michigan's industries built ships, bullets, engines, airplanes, and other equipment. Detroit was nicknamed the Arsenal of Democracy.

With so many men at war, Michigan's defense industries hired women and African American workers.

Unfortunately, this led to racial problems. In 1943, riots in Detroit left 34 dead and hundreds injured. In 1967, another Detroit riot was so out of control that the National Guard and the U.S. Army were called in. Racial issues continued for many years.

After days of rioting, a teenager hurries past National Guardsmen and a barbed wire blockade in Detroit in July 1967.

Did You Know?

The first factory to build aircraft on an assembly-line system was created in Michigan in 1942.

During World War II, auto-maker Henry Ford put his experience with mass production to good use. At a place called Willow Run near Ypsilanti, Michigan, a 3.5-million-square-foot (325,161-sq-m) airplane factory was built for making B-24 Liberator bombers. It was the largest manufacturing facility of its kind.

Charles Lindbergh, the first pilot to fly alone across the Atlantic Ocean, called the plant the Grand Canyon of the Mechanized World. Lindbergh worked as an aviation consultant for Ford.

Willow Run had a workforce of about 100,000 people. Many were women. Before this plant opened, a top California factory produced one B-24 bomber a day. At Willow Run, during peak production, a finished B-24 Liberator rolled off the assembly line every hour. By the time the war ended in 1945, it had produced a total of 8,685 Liberator bombers for the war effort.

Willow Run produced a total of 8,685 B-24 bombers for the war.

People

Henry Ford (1863-1947) created the Ford Motor Company in 1903. He pioneered mass production and assembly lines, which made cars affordable for most Americans. Ford believed that his workers should be able to own a car themselves. More than 15 million of his Model T cars were sold between 1908 and 1927. At that time, Ford's company was the largest car manufacturer in the world. Ford was from a successful farm family in the Dearborn area by Detroit. He worked as an apprentice machinist, sawmill operator, and engineer before turning to car manufacturing.

Will Keith (W.K.) Kellogg (1860-1951) was born in Battle Creek, Michigan. He and his brother, Dr. John Harvey Kellogg, believed in nutrition. In 1894, the two discovered the process to make flaked cereal. W.K. started his own cereal company in 1906, selling Kellogg's Toasted Corn Flakes. The greatly successful business became the Kellogg Company. Under W.K.'s leadership, Kellogg Company cereals were not only made and sold in the United States, but also Canada, Australia, and England. In 1930, W.K. used his wealth to help people. He created the W.K. Kellogg Foundation, giving away millions of dollars to charities.

Gerald Ford (1913-2006) grew up in Grand Rapids, becoming an Eagle Scout and a star player for the University of Michigan football team. Ford was a congressman for 25 years before becoming president of the United States from 1974 to 1977. Ford is the only president who was neither elected president nor vice president. In 1973, President Richard Nixon appointed Ford to be vice president. Ford replaced Vice President Spiro Agnew, who had resigned. The next year, Nixon himself resigned, and Ford became president. Ford ran for president in 1976, but lost to Jimmy Carter in a close election.

Madonna (1958-) is a talented singer, songwriter, actress, dancer, and film producer. She was born in Bay City. She has sold more than 200 million records worldwide. She has received both praise and criticism for her work. Her full name is Madonna Louise Ciccone.

Diana Ross (1944-) is an award-winning singer and songwriter from Detroit. In the 1960s, she was the lead singer of The Supremes. She later left to have a solo career. She became one of the most successful female recording artists of the 20th century, scoring many top-10 hits. Her music includes rhythm & blues, jazz, pop, soul, and disco.

Cities

Founded as a French post in 1701, **Detroit** is the largest city in Michigan. It is located on the Detroit River, a busy commercial waterway that connects Lake Erie with Lake Huron. The city was the state's first capital, but the government moved to Lansing in 1847.

Detroit is famous for its factories. It took the nickname Arsenal of Democracy during World War II, but is better known as The Motor City. Detroit is the home of Chrysler, Ford, and General Motors. In the early 1950s, the population of the city came close to 2 million people, but is now estimated at only 916,952.

Grand Rapids is the second-largest city in Michigan, with a population of 193,627. It is known as a leader in furniture

production. The office furniture companies of American Seating, Steelcase, and Herman Miller are headquartered here. In addition, there are automotive, aerospace, insurance, publishing, and health care businesses, as well as several colleges and universities.

Grand Rapids has a history of new ideas. In 1880, hydroelectric power was used to power storefront lights. The first regular-scheduled airline service began here in 1926. And, it was the first city to add fluoride to its drinking water in 1945 to help prevent tooth decay.

Lansing became Michigan's capital in 1847. Centrally located in the Lower Peninsula, Lansing has a population of 114,947. The city has many manufacturing, health care, insurance, and technology companies. Lansing is also home to Michigan State University.

Kalamazoo is in the southwestern part of Michigan's Lower Peninsula. The city has a population of 72,637. Several biotechnology companies are in Kalamazoo, including drug-maker Pfizer. The city is home to Western Michigan University and Kalamazoo College. Theaters, orchestras, museums, and several minor-league sports teams are also found in Kalamazoo.

Sault Sainte Marie, also called "the Soo," is the oldest city in Michigan. Located by the rapids of the St. Mary's River, it was founded in 1668. Today, its population is 14,005. Another city by the same name is on the other side of the river in Ontario, Canada. They were originally governed as one, but have been on different sides of the international border since 1797.

Tourism is the area's largest industry. People come to see the Soo Locks. Massive 1,000-foot (305-m) freighters move between the Great Lakes with huge cargoes of grain, coal, and iron. Part of the St. Lawrence Seaway, the canal is one of the busiest in the world.

Transportation

From the time of the birchbark canoes, the Great Lakes and connecting waterways have provided a way to move freight and people. The Soo Locks and Detroit River are very busy during the shipping season. Lakers and ocean-going freighters carry immense amounts of cargo. Two ferry lines transport passengers and vehicles across Lake Michigan.

The Mackinac Bridge is 5 miles (8 km) long.

Since Michigan is famous for building automobiles, it is no surprise that many roads crisscross the state. Interstates I-69 and I-75 run north and south, while I-94 and I-96 run east and west.

The first railroads in Michigan began operating in the mid-1830s. Today, railroads provide important transportation services. Most are freight trains, but Amtrak also runs daily passenger trains.

The Detroit Metropolitan Wayne County Airport is one of the busiest airports in the United States. It serves nearly 36 million passengers each year.

The Detroit Metropolitan Wayne County Airport is one of the busiest airports in the country.

Natural Resources

Michigan's farms make almost $6 billion in business each year. Farms are mainly located in the southern part of the state, where the soil and climate are most favorable. The largest farm income comes from dairy, corn, and soybeans. Many flowers and plants are also grown. The state has a major crop of apples, cherries, and blueberries.

Michigan was once the nation's top producer of lumber. By the early 1900s, whole regions had been cut. Today, the forests have regrown. Lumbering continues, with better forest conservation practices. The state has become one of the nation's top producers of Christmas trees.

Copper mining in the state began in earnest in 1840. Until the late 1880s, Michigan led the nation in copper production. However, its deep shaft mines were expensive to operate. Michigan's last copper mine closed in 1997.

Iron mining continues in the Upper Peninsula. In 2007, nearly 13 million tons (11.8 million metric tons) of ore came out of the Empire and Tilden Mines. Coal, limestone, gold, gypsum, salt, silver, slate, and limestone are also mined in Michigan.

The Empire Iron Mine in Michigan's Upper Peninsula is one of the largest producers of iron ore pellets in the world.

Industry

Many car builders are in Michigan.

Automobile engineering and manufacturing is Michigan's main industry. Chrysler, Ford, and General Motors are headquartered in the state. There are also many manufacturers who support the car makers. With so many businesses centered on the auto industry, the fortunes of the state largely rise and fall with its car business.

Unfortunately, American automotive companies face increased competition and costs. This has affected Michigan's economy. The state's unemployment rate is currently among the highest in the nation. However, there is still hope for Michigan's auto business. It is committed to remaining an industry leader, and has recovered from severe downturns in the past.

Successful efforts have been made to increase the variety of businesses in the state. Technology, defense, medical, and chemical manufacturers have companies in Michigan. The state's long tradition of furniture production continues with La-Z-Boy, Steelcase, and others.

A La-Z-Boy recliner.

Battle Creek is known as the Cereal City. It is home to the Kellogg Company and Post Cereals.

Tourism in Michigan is a multi-billion-dollar industry, employing nearly 200,000 people. It is a year-round business, and one of the state's largest income producers.

Battle Creek, Michigan, is nicknamed the Cereal City. It is home to the Kellogg Company and Post Cereals.

Sports

Michigan has vast forests, interesting state parks, and beautiful wilderness areas. These attract many campers, hikers, bikers, fishermen, and hunters.

A kayaker paddles past a lighthouse at St. Ignace, Michigan.

With four Great Lakes, 11,000 inland lakes and 36,000 miles (57,936 km) of rivers and streams, many of Michigan's recreation activities center on water. There are almost one million recreational boats in the state. Sport fishing, sailboat racing, canoeing, kayaking, swimming, and scuba diving are very popular.

Winter brings out downhill skiers and snowboarders. People also enjoy cross-country skiing, snowshoeing, ice-skating, and snowmobiling.

Michigan has many professional sports teams based out of the Detroit area. They include the National Football League's Detroit Lions, Major League Baseball's Detroit Tigers, the National Basketball Association's Detroit Pistons, the Women's National Basketball Association's Detroit Shock, and the National Hockey League's Detroit Red Wings. Professional hockey actually got its start in Michigan in 1902. The first team was organized at Portage Lake on the Keweenaw Peninsula, and the first professional league began playing in 1904.

Entertainment

Detroit, nicknamed Motown, is famous for its rhythm-and-blues music. The list of famous musicians who have called Michigan home includes Alice Cooper, Eminem, Aretha Franklin, John Lee Hooker, Kid Rock, Ted Nugent, Diana Ross, Smokey Robinson, Bob Seger, and Stevie Wonder.

It is no surprise that in a state with many automobile manufacturers, car racing is very popular. There are more than 30 tracks. The Michigan

Michigan International Speedway opened in 1968.

International Speedway in Brooklyn is a 2-mile (3.2-km) oval track mostly used for NASCAR events.

The annual North American International Auto Show has been held in Detroit since 1907. It is here that carmakers introduce new models to the public.

Some of the best car museums in the nation are found in Michigan.

Detroit's historic Fox Theatre is the second-largest theater in the country. With more than 5,000 seats, the beautiful theater hosts performances and movies.

The Gerald R. Ford Presidential Museum is the final resting place of the 38th president of the United States.

The Gerald R. Ford Presidential Museum is in Grand Rapids.

Michigan's Detroit Zoo was the first to feature wildlife in open spaces, allowing the animals more freedom.

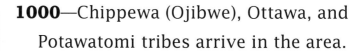

Timeline

1000—Chippewa (Ojibwe), Ottawa, and Potawatomi tribes arrive in the area.

Griffin

1618—Frenchman Etienne Brule explores the area around Lake Superior.

1667—The *Griffin* is the first large ship to sail on the Great Lakes.

1701—Frenchman Cadillac founds Detroit.

1835—The Toledo War, a territory conflict between Ohio and Michigan, is resolved by President Jackson and the U.S. Congress.

1837—Michigan becomes the 26th state.

1847—Lansing replaces Detroit as the capital.

1855—The Soo Locks open at Sault Ste. Marie.

1861-65—Michigan sends 90,000 troops to serve in the Union army.

1888—Michigan's lumber production peaks.

1908—Ford introduces his Model T automobile.

1941-45—During World War II, Michigan companies build military weapons and vehicles. Detroit is nicknamed the Arsenal of Democracy.

1943—Race riots in Detroit kill 34.

1957—The Mackinac Bridge is completed.

1967—Army and National Guard units are called in to help with Detroit race riots.

2008—Detroit Red Wings win the Stanley Cup.

Glossary

Boreal Forest—A forest usually found in a northern climate. It is filled with evergreen trees such as spruce, fir, and pine.

Erie Canal—A 360-mile (579-km) -long waterway running across New York state to Lake Erie. Opened in 1825, people and supplies could then be transported inland. This greatly helped with the settlement of the American Midwest.

Gale—A very strong wind, often accompanied by a storm.

Glacier—A huge, slow-moving sheet of ice that grows and shrinks as the climate changes. The ice sheets can be more than one mile (1.6 km) thick.

Lake Effect Snow—Winter weather systems pick up water over the Great Lakes. In the cold, it falls as heavy snow as far as 20 miles (32 km) inland.

Motown—Both a nickname for Detroit (Motor Town) and a style of rhythm-and-blues music developed in the city.

Purple Gang—A ruthless gang that stole smuggled shipments of alcohol from Canada, usually killing all witnesses. The gang controlled the Detroit underworld until about 1935.

Sedimentary Rock—Rock that is formed by a slow process of pressing together small particles.

St. Lawrence Seaway—A waterway between the United States and Canada that allows ships to travel from the Atlantic Ocean to the Great Lakes.

Underground Railroad—In the early 1800s, people created the Underground Railroad to help African Americans escape from slave states. It was a secret network of safe houses and connecting routes that led slaves to freedom.

World War I—A war that was fought in Europe from 1914 to 1918, involving countries around the world. The United States entered the war in April 1917.

World War II—A conflict across the world, lasting from 1939-1945. The United States entered the war in December 1941.

Index

MICHIGAN